This Practice Journal Belongs To:

Name _____

Phone _____

Email _____

Practice Journal Year

_____

WE NEED YOUR HELP!

We are a small business, and honest feedback and reviews from customers like you really make a difference. We would be honored if you would spread the word about our products by leaving a review on Amazon!

The Music Student's
Practice Journal

Tracking Your Artistry for Success

Olivia Ellis and Davis Dorrough

ISBN: 9798676079307

Music Goals

Long-term Goals

This practice journal is designed for an entire year of music making. Take a moment to **write down three long-term goals** for the coming year. These could be very specific goals such as preparing music for an upcoming performance, or they could be broader goals that focus on weak areas. Would you like to improve your technique, perform with more confidence, learn a specific piece, or become a better sight reader? Research has proven that writing down your aspirations will give you an advantage when it comes to achieving them!

Goal **1** _____

_____

_____

Goal **2** _____

_____

_____

Goal **3** _____

_____

_____

Achievement Plan

Now that you've taken the time to write down your long-term goals, let's go a step further and **list three action steps** you can take in order to get closer to reaching these goals.

For example, if my goal is to perform with more confidence, my action steps might include:

a. participate in five informal public performances this year
b. develop a pre-performance routine that centers my mind and body
c. learn practice techniques that will help me be prepared for performances

Choose anything you like for your action steps but make sure that they are things that could directly move you closer toward reaching your goals.

Steps for Goal 1

a. _____

b. _____

c. _____

Steps for Goal 2

a. _____

b. _____

c. _____

Steps for Goal 3

a. _____

b. _____

c. _____

Memory Goals

If you have upcoming performances that require memorization, this section is devoted to helping you set deadlines that will ensure you are prepared well in advance of performance dates. You can use this page to set goals for whole pieces or smaller passages.

1. _____ Date _____ ☐

2. _____ Date _____ ☐

3. _____ Date _____ ☐

4. _____ Date _____ ☐

5. _____ Date _____ ☐

6. _____ Date _____ ☐

7. _____ Date _____ ☐

8. _____ Date _____ ☐

9. _____ Date _____ ☐

10. _____ Date _____ ☐

Weekly Practice Assignment

Today's Date: 8 / 24 / 20

TECHNIQUE GOALS:

- White-key harmonic minor scales hands together
- Work on clarity in the left hand
- Practice in rhythms and staccato - ♩ = 88

REPERTOIRE GOALS:

- Chopin Waltz - Work on balance of melody and accompaniment. Shaping of phrases. Check notes in m. 27
- Bach Invention - Listen for clear entrances of motive. Watch out for articulations in m. 12

MUSIC THEORY:

pp. 8-9

OTHER REMINDERS:

- The slower you practice, the faster you'll get there!
- Studio class performance on September 12

Write your practice times or use check
marks for specific time increments

Student Practice Log

	TIME PRACTICED									DAILY TOTAL
DAY ❶	20 m									20 m
DAY ❷	10 m	5 m	20 m							35 m
DAY ❸	20 m	10 m	10 m							40 m
DAY ❹										
DAY ❺	✓	✓								30 m
DAY ❻	✓	✓	✓							45 m
DAY ❼	✓	✓								30 m

WEEKLY TOTAL: __3 hrs 20 m__

Did you achieve your practice goals? Circle one: (YES)   NO

PRACTICE REFLECTION:

I didn't get to practice on Wednesday, but I finished all of the
waltz. I really like this piece because of the beautiful melodies and
minor key sound. I listened to the recording you sent on YouTube and
noticed how expressively the performer played. She really moved
with the music! There were lots of soft dynamics. I am going to play
this piece for the studio class and need to work on that!

QUESTIONS FOR THE TEACHER:

I'm having trouble playing the 16th notes in Bach.

Can you help with my memory of Chopin?

Weekly Practice Assignment

Today's Date: /   /

TECHNIQUE GOALS:

REPERTOIRE GOALS:

MUSIC THEORY:

OTHER REMINDERS:

Student Practice Log

	TIME PRACTICED								DAILY TOTAL
DAY ❶									
DAY ❷									
DAY ❸									
DAY ❹									
DAY ❺									
DAY ❻									
DAY ❼									

WEEKLY TOTAL:_____

Did you achieve your practice goals? Circle one: YES   NO

PRACTICE REFLECTION:

QUESTIONS FOR THE TEACHER:

Weekly Practice Assignment

Today's Date: /   /

TECHNIQUE GOALS:

REPERTOIRE GOALS:

MUSIC THEORY:

OTHER REMINDERS:

Student Practice Log

	TIME PRACTICED								DAILY TOTAL
DAY ❶									
DAY ❷									
DAY ❸									
DAY ❹									
DAY ❺									
DAY ❻									
DAY ❼									

WEEKLY TOTAL: _____

Did you achieve your practice goals? Circle one: YES   NO

PRACTICE REFLECTION:

QUESTIONS FOR THE TEACHER:

Weekly Practice Assignment

Today's Date: / /

TECHNIQUE GOALS:

REPERTOIRE GOALS:

MUSIC THEORY:

OTHER REMINDERS:

Student Practice Log

	TIME PRACTICED								DAILY TOTAL
DAY ❶									
DAY ❷									
DAY ❸									
DAY ❹									
DAY ❺									
DAY ❻									
DAY ❼									

WEEKLY TOTAL:_____

Did you achieve your practice goals? Circle one: YES   NO

PRACTICE REFLECTION:

QUESTIONS FOR THE TEACHER:

Weekly Practice Assignment

Today's Date: /   /

TECHNIQUE GOALS:

REPERTOIRE GOALS:

MUSIC THEORY:

OTHER REMINDERS:

Student Practice Log

	TIME PRACTICED								DAILY TOTAL
DAY ❶									
DAY ❷									
DAY ❸									
DAY ❹									
DAY ❺									
DAY ❻									
DAY ❼									

WEEKLY TOTAL:_____

Did you achieve your practice goals? Circle one: YES   NO

PRACTICE REFLECTION:

QUESTIONS FOR THE TEACHER:

Weekly Practice Assignment

Today's Date: / /

TECHNIQUE GOALS:

REPERTOIRE GOALS:

MUSIC THEORY:

OTHER REMINDERS:

Student Practice Log

	TIME PRACTICED								DAILY TOTAL
DAY ❶									
DAY ❷									
DAY ❸									
DAY ❹									
DAY ❺									
DAY ❻									
DAY ❼									

WEEKLY TOTAL: _____

Did you achieve your practice goals? Circle one: YES   NO

PRACTICE REFLECTION:

QUESTIONS FOR THE TEACHER:

Weekly Practice Assignment

Today's Date: / /

TECHNIQUE GOALS:

REPERTOIRE GOALS:

MUSIC THEORY:

OTHER REMINDERS:

Student Practice Log

	TIME PRACTICED								DAILY TOTAL
DAY **1**									
DAY **2**									
DAY **3**									
DAY **4**									
DAY **5**									
DAY **6**									
DAY **7**									

WEEKLY TOTAL: _____

Did you achieve your practice goals? Circle one: YES   NO

PRACTICE REFLECTION:

QUESTIONS FOR THE TEACHER:

Weekly Practice Assignment

Today's Date: / /

TECHNIQUE GOALS:

REPERTOIRE GOALS:

MUSIC THEORY:

OTHER REMINDERS:

Student Practice Log

	TIME PRACTICED								DAILY TOTAL
DAY **1**									
DAY **2**									
DAY **3**									
DAY **4**									
DAY **5**									
DAY **6**									
DAY **7**									

WEEKLY TOTAL: _____

Did you achieve your practice goals? Circle one: YES   NO

PRACTICE REFLECTION:

QUESTIONS FOR THE TEACHER:

Weekly Practice Assignment

Today's Date: ___ / ___ / ___

TECHNIQUE GOALS:

REPERTOIRE GOALS:

MUSIC THEORY:

OTHER REMINDERS:

Student Practice Log

	TIME PRACTICED								DAILY TOTAL
DAY ❶									
DAY ❷									
DAY ❸									
DAY ❹									
DAY ❺									
DAY ❻									
DAY ❼									

WEEKLY TOTAL:_____

Did you achieve your practice goals? Circle one: YES   NO

PRACTICE REFLECTION:

QUESTIONS FOR THE TEACHER:

Weekly Practice Assignment

Today's Date: /   /

TECHNIQUE GOALS:

REPERTOIRE GOALS:

MUSIC THEORY:

OTHER REMINDERS:

Student Practice Log

	TIME PRACTICED								DAILY TOTAL
DAY ❶									
DAY ❷									
DAY ❸									
DAY ❹									
DAY ❺									
DAY ❻									
DAY ❼									

WEEKLY TOTAL: _____

Did you achieve your practice goals? Circle one: YES   NO

PRACTICE REFLECTION:

QUESTIONS FOR THE TEACHER:

Weekly Practice Assignment

Today's Date: / /

TECHNIQUE GOALS:

REPERTOIRE GOALS:

MUSIC THEORY:

OTHER REMINDERS:

Student Practice Log

	TIME PRACTICED								DAILY TOTAL
DAY **1**									
DAY **2**									
DAY **3**									
DAY **4**									
DAY **5**									
DAY **6**									
DAY **7**									

WEEKLY TOTAL: _____

Did you achieve your practice goals? Circle one: YES   NO

PRACTICE REFLECTION:

QUESTIONS FOR THE TEACHER:

Weekly Practice Assignment

Today's Date: /   /

TECHNIQUE GOALS:

REPERTOIRE GOALS:

MUSIC THEORY:

OTHER REMINDERS:

Student Practice Log

	TIME PRACTICED								DAILY TOTAL
DAY **1**									
DAY **2**									
DAY **3**									
DAY **4**									
DAY **5**									
DAY **6**									
DAY **7**									

WEEKLY TOTAL: _____

Did you achieve your practice goals? Circle one: YES   NO

PRACTICE REFLECTION:

QUESTIONS FOR THE TEACHER:

Weekly Practice Assignment

Today's Date: /   /

TECHNIQUE GOALS:

REPERTOIRE GOALS:

MUSIC THEORY:

OTHER REMINDERS:

Student Practice Log

	TIME PRACTICED								DAILY TOTAL
DAY ❶									
DAY ❷									
DAY ❸									
DAY ❹									
DAY ❺									
DAY ❻									
DAY ❼									

WEEKLY TOTAL:_____

Did you achieve your practice goals? Circle one: YES   NO

PRACTICE REFLECTION:

QUESTIONS FOR THE TEACHER:

Weekly Practice Assignment

Today's Date: /   /

TECHNIQUE GOALS:

REPERTOIRE GOALS:

MUSIC THEORY:

OTHER REMINDERS:

Student Practice Log

	TIME PRACTICED								DAILY TOTAL
DAY ❶									
DAY ❷									
DAY ❸									
DAY ❹									
DAY ❺									
DAY ❻									
DAY ❼									

WEEKLY TOTAL:_____

Did you achieve your practice goals? Circle one: YES   NO

PRACTICE REFLECTION:

QUESTIONS FOR THE TEACHER:

Weekly Practice Assignment

Today's Date: /   /

TECHNIQUE GOALS:

REPERTOIRE GOALS:

MUSIC THEORY:

OTHER REMINDERS:

Student Practice Log

	TIME PRACTICED								DAILY TOTAL
DAY ❶									
DAY ❷									
DAY ❸									
DAY ❹									
DAY ❺									
DAY ❻									
DAY ❼									

WEEKLY TOTAL:_____

Did you achieve your practice goals? Circle one: YES   NO

PRACTICE REFLECTION:

QUESTIONS FOR THE TEACHER:

Weekly Practice Assignment

Today's Date: /   /

TECHNIQUE GOALS:

REPERTOIRE GOALS:

MUSIC THEORY:

OTHER REMINDERS:

Student Practice Log

	TIME PRACTICED							DAILY TOTAL
DAY **1**								
DAY **2**								
DAY **3**								
DAY **4**								
DAY **5**								
DAY **6**								
DAY **7**								

WEEKLY TOTAL: _____

Did you achieve your practice goals? Circle one: YES   NO

PRACTICE REFLECTION:

QUESTIONS FOR THE TEACHER:

Weekly Practice Assignment

Today's Date: /   /

TECHNIQUE GOALS:

REPERTOIRE GOALS:

MUSIC THEORY:

OTHER REMINDERS:

Student Practice Log

	TIME PRACTICED								DAILY TOTAL
DAY ❶									
DAY ❷									
DAY ❸									
DAY ❹									
DAY ❺									
DAY ❻									
DAY ❼									

WEEKLY TOTAL:_____

Did you achieve your practice goals? Circle one: YES   NO

PRACTICE REFLECTION:

QUESTIONS FOR THE TEACHER:

Weekly Practice Assignment

Today's Date: /   /

TECHNIQUE GOALS:

REPERTOIRE GOALS:

MUSIC THEORY:

OTHER REMINDERS:

Student Practice Log

	TIME PRACTICED							DAILY TOTAL
DAY ❶								
DAY ❷								
DAY ❸								
DAY ❹								
DAY ❺								
DAY ❻								
DAY ❼								

WEEKLY TOTAL:_____

Did you achieve your practice goals? Circle one: YES   NO

PRACTICE REFLECTION:

QUESTIONS FOR THE TEACHER:

Weekly Practice Assignment

Today's Date: /   /

TECHNIQUE GOALS:

REPERTOIRE GOALS:

MUSIC THEORY:

OTHER REMINDERS:

Student Practice Log

	TIME PRACTICED								DAILY TOTAL
DAY ❶									
DAY ❷									
DAY ❸									
DAY ❹									
DAY ❺									
DAY ❻									
DAY ❼									

WEEKLY TOTAL:_____

Did you achieve your practice goals? Circle one: YES   NO

PRACTICE REFLECTION:

QUESTIONS FOR THE TEACHER:

Weekly Practice Assignment

Today's Date: / /

TECHNIQUE GOALS:

REPERTOIRE GOALS:

MUSIC THEORY:

OTHER REMINDERS:

Student Practice Log

	TIME PRACTICED							DAILY TOTAL
DAY ❶								
DAY ❷								
DAY ❸								
DAY ❹								
DAY ❺								
DAY ❻								
DAY ❼								

WEEKLY TOTAL: _____

Did you achieve your practice goals? Circle one: YES   NO

PRACTICE REFLECTION:

QUESTIONS FOR THE TEACHER:

Weekly Practice Assignment

Today's Date: _____ / _____ / _____

TECHNIQUE GOALS:

REPERTOIRE GOALS:

MUSIC THEORY:

OTHER REMINDERS:

Student Practice Log

	TIME PRACTICED								DAILY TOTAL
DAY ❶									
DAY ❷									
DAY ❸									
DAY ❹									
DAY ❺									
DAY ❻									
DAY ❼									

WEEKLY TOTAL:_____

Did you achieve your practice goals? Circle one: YES   NO

PRACTICE REFLECTION:

QUESTIONS FOR THE TEACHER:

Weekly Practice Assignment

Today's Date: ___ / ___ / ___

TECHNIQUE GOALS:

REPERTOIRE GOALS:

MUSIC THEORY:

OTHER REMINDERS:

Student Practice Log

	TIME PRACTICED								DAILY TOTAL
DAY **1**									
DAY **2**									
DAY **3**									
DAY **4**									
DAY **5**									
DAY **6**									
DAY **7**									

WEEKLY TOTAL:_____

Did you achieve your practice goals? Circle one: YES   NO

PRACTICE REFLECTION:

QUESTIONS FOR THE TEACHER:

Weekly Practice Assignment

Today's Date: /   /

TECHNIQUE GOALS:

REPERTOIRE GOALS:

MUSIC THEORY:

OTHER REMINDERS:

Student Practice Log

	TIME PRACTICED							DAILY TOTAL
DAY **1**								
DAY **2**								
DAY **3**								
DAY **4**								
DAY **5**								
DAY **6**								
DAY **7**								

WEEKLY TOTAL:_____

Did you achieve your practice goals? Circle one: YES   NO

PRACTICE REFLECTION:

QUESTIONS FOR THE TEACHER:

Weekly Practice Assignment

Today's Date: / /

TECHNIQUE GOALS:

REPERTOIRE GOALS:

MUSIC THEORY:

OTHER REMINDERS:

Student Practice Log

	TIME PRACTICED								DAILY TOTAL
DAY 1									
DAY 2									
DAY 3									
DAY 4									
DAY 5									
DAY 6									
DAY 7									

WEEKLY TOTAL: _____

Did you achieve your practice goals? Circle one: YES   NO

PRACTICE REFLECTION:

QUESTIONS FOR THE TEACHER:

Weekly Practice Assignment

Today's Date: /   /

TECHNIQUE GOALS:

REPERTOIRE GOALS:

MUSIC THEORY:

OTHER REMINDERS:

Student Practice Log

	TIME PRACTICED								DAILY TOTAL
DAY **1**									
DAY **2**									
DAY **3**									
DAY **4**									
DAY **5**									
DAY **6**									
DAY **7**									

WEEKLY TOTAL: _____

Did you achieve your practice goals? Circle one: YES   NO

PRACTICE REFLECTION:

QUESTIONS FOR THE TEACHER:

Weekly Practice Assignment

Today's Date: / /

TECHNIQUE GOALS:

REPERTOIRE GOALS:

MUSIC THEORY:

OTHER REMINDERS:

Student Practice Log

	TIME PRACTICED								DAILY TOTAL
DAY ❶									
DAY ❷									
DAY ❸									
DAY ❹									
DAY ❺									
DAY ❻									
DAY ❼									

WEEKLY TOTAL:_____

Did you achieve your practice goals? Circle one: YES   NO

PRACTICE REFLECTION:

QUESTIONS FOR THE TEACHER:

Weekly Practice Assignment

Today's Date: /   /

TECHNIQUE GOALS:

REPERTOIRE GOALS:

MUSIC THEORY:

OTHER REMINDERS:

Student Practice Log

	TIME PRACTICED								DAILY TOTAL
DAY ❶									
DAY ❷									
DAY ❸									
DAY ❹									
DAY ❺									
DAY ❻									
DAY ❼									

WEEKLY TOTAL:_____

Did you achieve your practice goals? Circle one: YES   NO

PRACTICE REFLECTION:

QUESTIONS FOR THE TEACHER:

Weekly Practice Assignment

Today's Date: / /

TECHNIQUE GOALS:

REPERTOIRE GOALS:

MUSIC THEORY:

OTHER REMINDERS:

Student Practice Log

	TIME PRACTICED								DAILY TOTAL
DAY ❶									
DAY ❷									
DAY ❸									
DAY ❹									
DAY ❺									
DAY ❻									
DAY ❼									

WEEKLY TOTAL: _____

Did you achieve your practice goals? Circle one: YES   NO

PRACTICE REFLECTION:

QUESTIONS FOR THE TEACHER:

Weekly Practice Assignment

Today's Date: /   /

TECHNIQUE GOALS:

REPERTOIRE GOALS:

MUSIC THEORY:

OTHER REMINDERS:

Student Practice Log

	TIME PRACTICED								DAILY TOTAL
DAY ❶									
DAY ❷									
DAY ❸									
DAY ❹									
DAY ❺									
DAY ❻									
DAY ❼									

WEEKLY TOTAL:_____

Did you achieve your practice goals? Circle one: YES   NO

PRACTICE REFLECTION:

QUESTIONS FOR THE TEACHER:

Weekly Practice Assignment

Today's Date: /   /

TECHNIQUE GOALS:

REPERTOIRE GOALS:

MUSIC THEORY:

OTHER REMINDERS:

Student Practice Log

	TIME PRACTICED								DAILY TOTAL
DAY ❶									
DAY ❷									
DAY ❸									
DAY ❹									
DAY ❺									
DAY ❻									
DAY ❼									

WEEKLY TOTAL:_____

Did you achieve your practice goals? Circle one: YES   NO

PRACTICE REFLECTION:

QUESTIONS FOR THE TEACHER:

Weekly Practice Assignment

Today's Date: / /

TECHNIQUE GOALS:

REPERTOIRE GOALS:

MUSIC THEORY:

OTHER REMINDERS:

Student Practice Log

	TIME PRACTICED								DAILY TOTAL
DAY **1**									
DAY **2**									
DAY **3**									
DAY **4**									
DAY **5**									
DAY **6**									
DAY **7**									

WEEKLY TOTAL: _____

Did you achieve your practice goals? Circle one: YES   NO

PRACTICE REFLECTION:

QUESTIONS FOR THE TEACHER:

Weekly Practice Assignment

Today's Date: / /

TECHNIQUE GOALS:

REPERTOIRE GOALS:

MUSIC THEORY:

OTHER REMINDERS:

Student Practice Log

	TIME PRACTICED								DAILY TOTAL
DAY ❶									
DAY ❷									
DAY ❸									
DAY ❹									
DAY ❺									
DAY ❻									
DAY ❼									

WEEKLY TOTAL: _____

Did you achieve your practice goals? Circle one: YES   NO

PRACTICE REFLECTION:

QUESTIONS FOR THE TEACHER:

Weekly Practice Assignment

Today's Date: /   /

TECHNIQUE GOALS:

REPERTOIRE GOALS:

MUSIC THEORY:

OTHER REMINDERS:

Student Practice Log

	TIME PRACTICED								DAILY TOTAL
DAY ❶									
DAY ❷									
DAY ❸									
DAY ❹									
DAY ❺									
DAY ❻									
DAY ❼									

WEEKLY TOTAL: _____

Did you achieve your practice goals? Circle one: YES   NO

PRACTICE REFLECTION:

QUESTIONS FOR THE TEACHER:

Weekly Practice Assignment

Today's Date: / /

TECHNIQUE GOALS:

REPERTOIRE GOALS:

MUSIC THEORY:

OTHER REMINDERS:

Student Practice Log

	TIME PRACTICED								DAILY TOTAL
DAY ❶									
DAY ❷									
DAY ❸									
DAY ❹									
DAY ❺									
DAY ❻									
DAY ❼									

WEEKLY TOTAL: _____

Did you achieve your practice goals? Circle one: YES   NO

PRACTICE REFLECTION:

QUESTIONS FOR THE TEACHER:

Weekly Practice Assignment

Today's Date: / /

TECHNIQUE GOALS:

REPERTOIRE GOALS:

MUSIC THEORY:

OTHER REMINDERS:

Student Practice Log

	TIME PRACTICED							DAILY TOTAL
DAY ❶								
DAY ❷								
DAY ❸								
DAY ❹								
DAY ❺								
DAY ❻								
DAY ❼								

WEEKLY TOTAL: _____

Did you achieve your practice goals? Circle one: YES   NO

PRACTICE REFLECTION:

QUESTIONS FOR THE TEACHER:

Weekly Practice Assignment

Today's Date: / /

TECHNIQUE GOALS:

REPERTOIRE GOALS:

MUSIC THEORY:

OTHER REMINDERS:

Student Practice Log

	TIME PRACTICED								DAILY TOTAL
DAY ❶									
DAY ❷									
DAY ❸									
DAY ❹									
DAY ❺									
DAY ❻									
DAY ❼									

WEEKLY TOTAL: _____

Did you achieve your practice goals? Circle one: YES   NO

PRACTICE REFLECTION:

QUESTIONS FOR THE TEACHER:

Weekly Practice Assignment

Today's Date: /   /

TECHNIQUE GOALS:

REPERTOIRE GOALS:

MUSIC THEORY:

OTHER REMINDERS:

Student Practice Log

	TIME PRACTICED								DAILY TOTAL
DAY ❶									
DAY ❷									
DAY ❸									
DAY ❹									
DAY ❺									
DAY ❻									
DAY ❼									

WEEKLY TOTAL: _____

Did you achieve your practice goals? Circle one: YES   NO

PRACTICE REFLECTION:

QUESTIONS FOR THE TEACHER:

Weekly Practice Assignment

Today's Date: /   /

TECHNIQUE GOALS:

REPERTOIRE GOALS:

MUSIC THEORY:

OTHER REMINDERS:

Student Practice Log

	TIME PRACTICED							DAILY TOTAL
DAY ❶								
DAY ❷								
DAY ❸								
DAY ❹								
DAY ❺								
DAY ❻								
DAY ❼								

WEEKLY TOTAL: _____

Did you achieve your practice goals? Circle one: YES   NO

PRACTICE REFLECTION:

QUESTIONS FOR THE TEACHER:

Weekly Practice Assignment

Today's Date: /   /

TECHNIQUE GOALS:

REPERTOIRE GOALS:

MUSIC THEORY:

OTHER REMINDERS:

Student Practice Log

	TIME PRACTICED							DAILY TOTAL
DAY ❶								
DAY ❷								
DAY ❸								
DAY ❹								
DAY ❺								
DAY ❻								
DAY ❼								

WEEKLY TOTAL: _____

Did you achieve your practice goals? Circle one: YES   NO

PRACTICE REFLECTION:

QUESTIONS FOR THE TEACHER:

Weekly Practice Assignment

Today's Date: /   /

TECHNIQUE GOALS:

REPERTOIRE GOALS:

MUSIC THEORY:

OTHER REMINDERS:

Student Practice Log

	TIME PRACTICED								DAILY TOTAL
DAY **1**									
DAY **2**									
DAY **3**									
DAY **4**									
DAY **5**									
DAY **6**									
DAY **7**									

WEEKLY TOTAL: _____

Did you achieve your practice goals? Circle one: YES   NO

PRACTICE REFLECTION:

QUESTIONS FOR THE TEACHER:

Weekly Practice Assignment

Today's Date: /   /

TECHNIQUE GOALS:

REPERTOIRE GOALS:

MUSIC THEORY:

OTHER REMINDERS:

Student Practice Log

	TIME PRACTICED								DAILY TOTAL
DAY ❶									
DAY ❷									
DAY ❸									
DAY ❹									
DAY ❺									
DAY ❻									
DAY ❼									
WEEKLY TOTAL:_____									

Did you achieve your practice goals? Circle one: YES   NO

PRACTICE REFLECTION:

QUESTIONS FOR THE TEACHER:

Weekly Practice Assignment

Today's Date: / /

TECHNIQUE GOALS:

REPERTOIRE GOALS:

MUSIC THEORY:

OTHER REMINDERS:

Student Practice Log

	TIME PRACTICED								DAILY TOTAL
DAY **1**									
DAY **2**									
DAY **3**									
DAY **4**									
DAY **5**									
DAY **6**									
DAY **7**									

WEEKLY TOTAL:_____

Did you achieve your practice goals? Circle one: YES   NO

PRACTICE REFLECTION:

QUESTIONS FOR THE TEACHER:

Weekly Practice Assignment

Today's Date: / /

TECHNIQUE GOALS:

REPERTOIRE GOALS:

MUSIC THEORY:

OTHER REMINDERS:

Student Practice Log

	TIME PRACTICED								DAILY TOTAL
DAY ❶									
DAY ❷									
DAY ❸									
DAY ❹									
DAY ❺									
DAY ❻									
DAY ❼									

WEEKLY TOTAL: _____

Did you achieve your practice goals? Circle one: YES   NO

PRACTICE REFLECTION:

QUESTIONS FOR THE TEACHER:

Weekly Practice Assignment

Today's Date: / /

TECHNIQUE GOALS:

REPERTOIRE GOALS:

MUSIC THEORY:

OTHER REMINDERS:

Student Practice Log

	TIME PRACTICED							DAILY TOTAL
DAY **1**								
DAY **2**								
DAY **3**								
DAY **4**								
DAY **5**								
DAY **6**								
DAY **7**								

WEEKLY TOTAL:_____

Did you achieve your practice goals? Circle one: YES   NO

PRACTICE REFLECTION:

QUESTIONS FOR THE TEACHER:

Made in the USA
Monee, IL
05 December 2024

72352307R00057